TIME FOR KIDS

All Aboard! How Trains Work

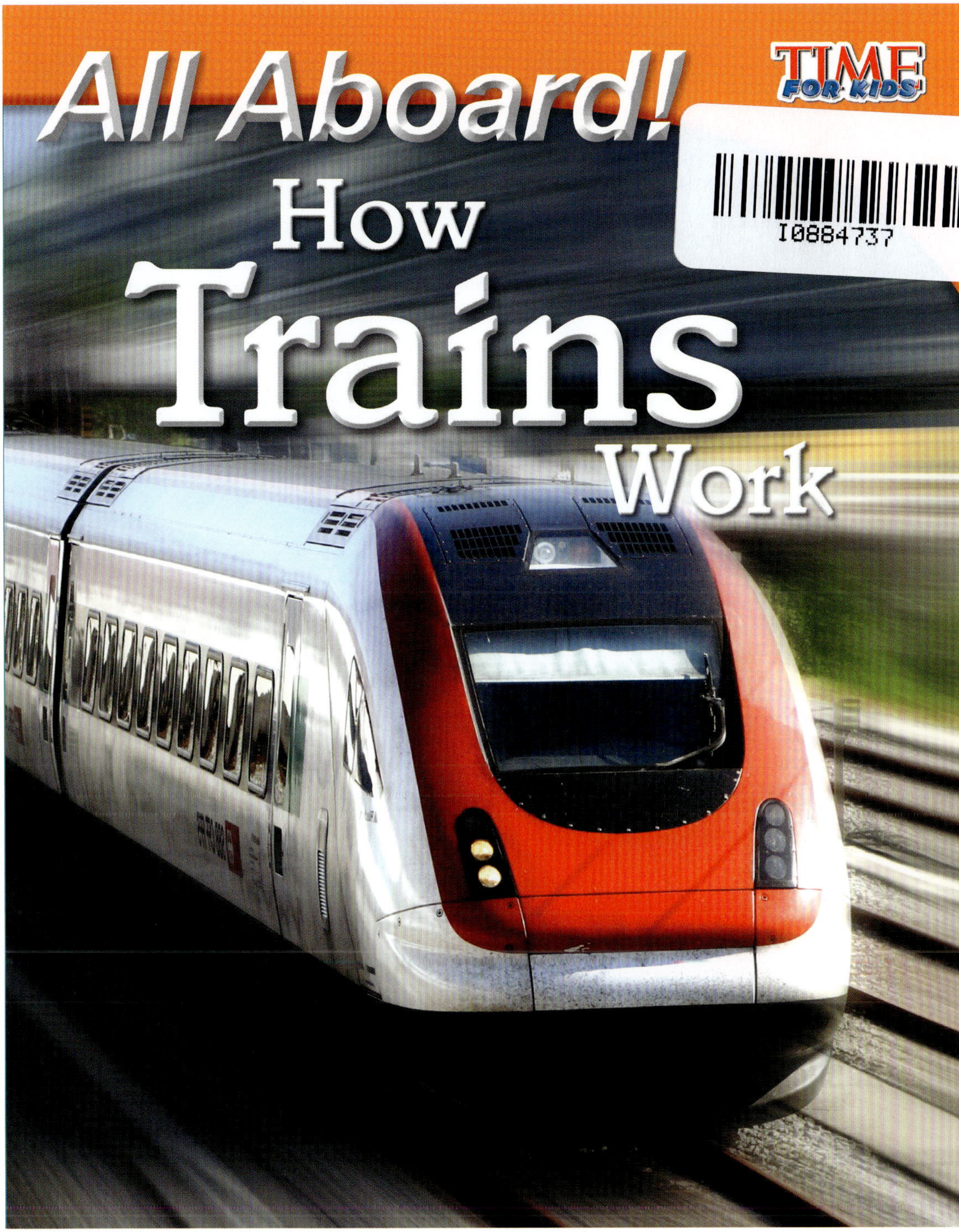

I0884737

Jennifer Prior

Consultants

Timothy Rasinski, Ph.D.
Kent State University

J.P. Naybor
Train Conductor

Morris E. Nelson
Railway Switchman

Publishing Credits

Dona Herweck Rice, *Editor-in-Chief*
Robin Erickson, *Production Director*
Lee Aucoin, *Creative Director*
Conni Medina, M.A.Ed., *Editorial Director*
Jamey Acosta, *Editor*
Heidi Kellenberger, *Editor*
Lexa Hoang, *Designer*
Stephanie Reid, *Photo Editor*
Rachelle Cracchiolo, M.S.Ed., *Publisher*

Image Credits
Cover hfng/Shutterstock; p.3 Maikloff/Shutterstock; p.4 jpbcpajpbcpa/iStockphoto; p.5 Kenneth Sponsler/iStockphoto; p.6 World History Archive/Newscom; p.8 LOC-LC-USZC4-9044; p.9 akg-images/Newscom; p.9 LOC-LC-D41-140; p.10 Rick Neese; p.11 left to right: Joe Belanger/Shutterstock; ollo/iStockphoto; p.12 The Print Collector/Alamy; p.13 FloridaStock/Shutterstock; p.14 Chris Curtis/Shutterstock; p.15 Oleksiy Mark/Shutterstock; p.16 Tim Pleasant/Dreamstime; p.17 top to bottom: akg-images/Newscom; AFP/Getty Images; p.18 left to right: Robert J. Beyers II/Shutterstock; Darryl Brooks/Shutterstock; p.19 Ulrich Mueller/Shutterstock; p.20 left to right: s_oleg/Shutterstock; Kenneth Sponsler/Shutterstock; p.21 top to bottom: BartlomiejMagierowski/Shutterstock; Condor 36/Shutterstock; p.22 top to bottom: DDCoral/Shutterstock; R Carner/Shutterstock; marekuliasz/Shutterstock; p.23 MARGRIT HIRSCH/Shutterstock; p.24 left to right: Yulia/BigStock; Fox Photos/Getty Images; p.25 top to bottom: Judy Tan; m11/ZUMA Press; p.26 AFP/Getty Images; p.28 Maikloff/Shutterstock; back cover: Maikloff/Shutterstock

Based on writing from *TIME For Kids.*

TIME For Kids and the *TIME For Kids* logo are registered trademarks of TIME Inc. Used under license.

Teacher Created Materials
5301 Oceanus Drive
Huntington Beach, CA 92649-1030
http://www.tcmpub.com

ISBN 978-1-4333-3656-0
© 2012 Teacher Created Materials, Inc.
Printed in China WAI002

Table of Contents

Train Song

A lonesome song floats through the air. "Woo, woo," it sounds in the distance. Then nearer and nearer it draws. "Clickety-clack, clickety-clack," the train calls as it moves closer along the track.

"Ding, ding, ding, ding, ding," sounds the bell at the crossing. Car after car chugs by. "Clickety-clack, clickety-clack." What is it carrying? Where is it going? "Clickety-clack, clickety-clack." What makes it move? How many miles will it travel? "Ding, ding, ding." The crossing bell falls silent. The train moves into the quiet night. A lonesome song floats in the distance, "Woo, woo…woo, woo…woo, woo."

Trains are used to transport many different things.

The Wabash Cannonball

In the late 1800s and early 1900s, railroad travel was the fastest way to go. People found it exciting to travel long distances by train. Some popular songs of the time show how they felt. Here is part of "The Wabash Cannonball," one of the most popular songs of the time.

Listen to the jingle, the rumble, and the roar,
As she glides along the woodlands, over
hills and by the shore.
Hear the mighty rush of the engine, hear the
lonesome whistle's call.
Traveling through the jungles on the Wabash
Cannonball.

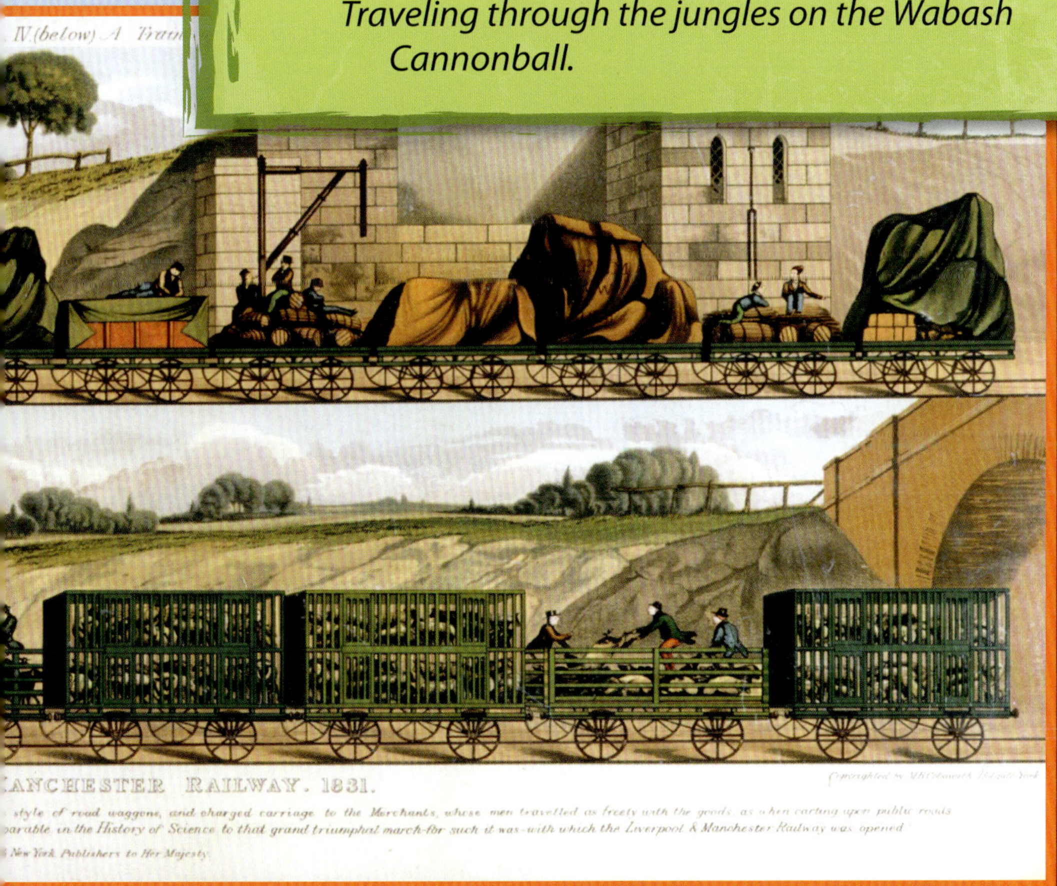

A Brief History of Trains

Trains were first used in the early 1800s. They were not like trains today. The cars were like wagons. They were pulled along tracks by horses.

In 1830, the first steam-powered train was run. After this, many railways were made. Most were short-run tracks. That means the tracks were not very long. They carried people and **freight**.

Later, long railways were made. Trains could travel across the country. They even had beds on them. This made the long trips easier for passengers.

advertisement for the first steam-powered train

Hop on the Train

The top year for train travel was 1920. But after that, the number of people traveling by train began to drop off as the numbers of automobiles increased. Today, train travel is growing in popularity again, perhaps to avoid automobile traffic and pollution.

Laying Track

In 1840, there were 2,818 miles of track in the United States. By 1860, there were 30,000 miles of track. In 1869, the first track reaching across the United States was completed. It was called the Transcontinental Railroad.

How Trains Work

The Rails

Trains run along tracks made of steel and wood. The rails are steel. Wooden **ties** hold them together. Long strips of steel are joined by steel joints. These are called **angle bars**. Angle bars cause the train to make a loud racket. The wheels of the train bump the **fishplates**. That makes the clickety-clack sound.

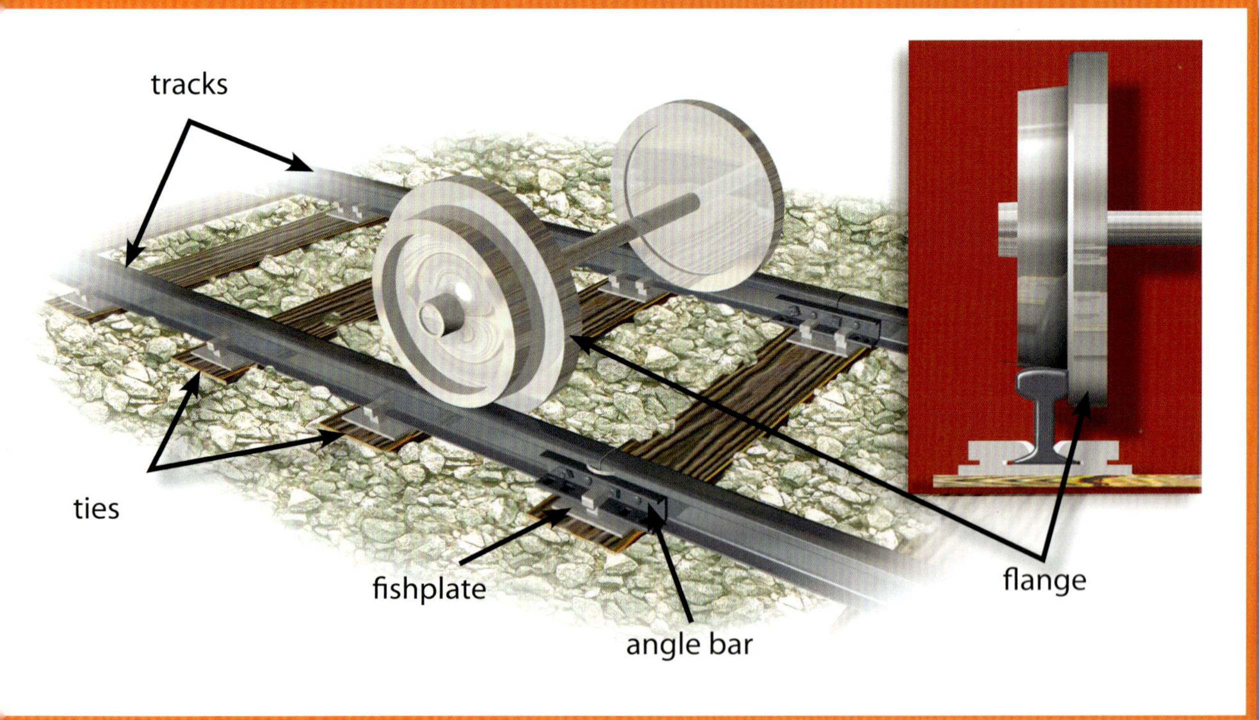

Trains run on tracks like those shown here.

The flange keeps the wheel on the track.

The Wheels

Train wheels are different from the wheels on cars. Each wheel has a **flange** (FLANJ) that fits over the inside of the track rail. The flange hugs the rail and keeps the train on the track. It does not need to be steered like a car.

Engines

Years ago, all trains had **steam engines**. Steam was forced into the engine. The steam moved rods connected to the wheels. The rods made the wheels turn.

Steam-powered trains got the name "choo-choo trains." When the engine steam was let go through a whistle, it made a choo-choo sound.

▲ This is what the inside of a steam engine looks like.

Another Word for *Train*

Choo-choo is one name for a train. *Locomotive* is another. *Loco* means "from a place." *Motive* means "causing motion." Together, locomotive means "moving from a place."

Today's trains run on electricity or diesel electricity. **Diesel-electric engines** are like huge truck engines. They run on fuel. The engine makes electricity, and electricity turns the wheels of the train.

Electric engines get their electricity from wires above them or special tracks below them. They are usually used for short distances because they are expensive to run.

What Is It?

Diesel (DEE-zuhl) is a type of heavy oil fuel.

How Fast?

The average train can go about 60 miles per hour. But, a special train called the French TGV goes at the average speed of 131 miles per hour. It also set the train-speed record at 320 miles per hour!

Working on the Train

Since a train is not driven like a car, does it drive itself? Certainly not! There are many workers on trains and in train yards who keep things running.

The **conductor** is in charge. He or she is like the captain of a team. The conductor makes all the decisions.

The **engineer** drives the train. Years ago, engineers fixed broken engines. Now, most engines can be repaired through their computer systems.

▼ A yard engine is a train that does work in the train yard.

The **brakemen** work on trains and in train yards. They **couple** and **uncouple** cars, **throw** switches, and much more. They stay very busy!

These workers train hard for their jobs. After all, it is their job to move people and supplies safely.

▲ The switchman is in charge of the brakes.

▼ The conductor is called a *foreman* when he is on a yard engine.

▼ The engineer drives the train.

Train Cars

Long ago, train cars were linked together with hooks. This caused problems. When the train stopped, the cars bumped together. Now, trains are connected with **couplers**. They keep the cars from crashing into one another.

◀ coupler

▼ boxcars

Think about the trains you have seen. Cars are made in different ways. Some trains carry people. Other train cars carry animals or supplies.

▲ auto train

Freight Cars

Most train cars are **freight cars**, which are used to move **cargo**. Different cars carry different kinds of cargo.

Boxcars are like big metal boxes. Each one has a roof and side walls. Some are refrigerated to carry food and other items that must stay cool.

Tank cars are often used to hold liquid. They usually carry fuel.

◀ tank car

▼ boxcar

Passenger Cars

Some trains carry people. People can eat, sleep, and move around in a **passenger car**. Dining cars are for eating meals. Sleeping cars have small rooms with beds. Observation cars allow people to look around. Baggage cars hold suitcases.

passenger car

dining car

hopper cars ▶

livestock cars ▶

Hopper cars can have an open or closed top. Each one has a dump door underneath. The door opens and the supply (such as grain or coal) dumps out.

Stock cars are used to carry animals. They allow fresh air to come inside. They have stalls for the animals.

Trains used to have **cabooses** attached to the end. This is where the conductor sat. He watched the back of the train. Today trains no longer need cabooses.

What Happened to the Caboose?

Today, most cabooses have been replaced with electric boxes that "watch" for trouble.

▼ caboose

Train Transportation

In the 1960s, people wanted a better way to travel. They worried about car pollution. Airports were sometimes too far away. So, train travel became popular again.

In the 1970s, **Amtrak** was created in the United States. Amtrak trains travel to over 500 destinations in 46 states. Millions of people ride on Amtrak trains every year.

Trains are the least expensive way to move cargo. Using trains instead of cars or trucks may reduce pollution, too.

The next time you hear that lonesome song in the distance, you may wonder, "Where are you going, old train? How many miles will you travel before your journey ends?"

sleeper cars

Commuter Trains

Commuter trains are special trains that people use for short distances, such as going back and forth from work. More and more people are traveling by commuter trains each year. That way, they can read, sleep, or work while they go!

All Aboard!

To travel by train, just look at a map and a schedule. Where do you want to go? A train can probably get you there!

The colored lines on the map show the train routes.

FROM	TO	DEPARTS	ARRIVES
St. Petersburg RUSSIA	Moscow RUSSIA	4:40 P.M. 10/12	3:55 A.M. 10/13
Moscow RUSSIA	Kiev UKRAINE	6:30 P.M. 10/13	6:35 P.M. 10/14

Glossary

Amtrak—a train system in the United States

angle bars—metal pieces that connect the rails of train tracks

boxcars—train cars that carry supplies

brakemen—workers on a train or in the train yard who do such tasks as coupling and uncoupling cars, throwing switches, and passing signals

cabooses—cars on older trains used to help stop the train

cargo—supplies or equipment carried on a train or other vehicle

conductor—the person who is in charge of the train crew and makes sure everything runs correctly and safely

couple—to attach train cars together

couplers—special metal pieces used to attach train cars together and keep them from running into one another

diesel-electric engines—very large engines on trains, run by diesel fuel and electricity

engineer—the person who drives a train

fishplates—the metal or wooden plates attached to the sides of two rails to connect them

flange—the inside rim of a train wheel that holds the wheel on the rail

freight—supplies or equipment carried on a train or other vehicle

freight cars—train cars that carry cargo

hopper cars—train cars that have doors underneath to release cargo

passenger car—a train car in which people can eat, sleep, and carry their belongings

steam engines—train engines that run on steam

stock cars—train cars that carry animals

tank cars—train cars that carry liquids

throw—to change or switch the direction of the tracks

ties—beams laid across railroad beds to connect the rails

uncouple—to disconnect train cars

Index